I can't talk

Copyright © 2024 Lisa Marie Wooding.

No part of this book may be reproduced or transmitted by any means, except as permitted by UK copyright law or the author. For licensing requests, please contact the author at lisawooding23@icloud.com

ISBN: 9798327759695

Images by Lisa Marie Wooding.
Book design through Canva.

Printed by Amazon KDP..

First printing edition 2024.

For Alexander, my breath of fresh air - you amaze me every day.

Introduction - a note for parents and carers

I decided that I wanted to write something not just about my son, but about all non-verbal children. My son is 4 years old; he's currently on the autistic pathway - a lot of parents will know the challenges and frustrations we face, not just from day-to-day life but the never-ending waiting lists, and the promise for support.

My son is amazing. It's taken some time, but we are in a great situation since he's learned Makaton and is guided by routine and visuals. He is a bubbly, beautiful, determined force of nature!

Although this little story is written for children, I believe it could be of some help to grown-ups too. Unfortunately, there is still a lot of ignorance around neurodiversity. This book shows the similarities between ALL people - just because someone doesn't have speech, it doesn't mean they can't put their view across, it doesn't mean they aren't intelligent, it doesn't mean they don't understand, and it certainly doesn't mean that they don't have feelings.

I hope this will be helpful in explaining things to your child, their siblings, and even wider family and friends.

And on a personal note, parenting a child with additional needs is not an easy journey, but you will always be your child's strongest advocate. Never give up, you know your child best.

I can't talk, but I can laugh.
I have a fantastic sense of humour.

I can't talk, but I can feel.
Sometimes I'm sad and angry. I can get frustrated
when people don't understand me.
Most of the time, I am happy.

I can't talk, but I can love.
My family make me so happy and I love squeezing my soft toys.

I can't talk, but I know everything about numbers.
I love to hear people count.

I can't talk, but I enjoy time outdoors.
Jumping in puddles is my favourite.

I can't talk, but I can listen.
Music calms me down.

I can't talk, but I understand.
I understand instructions and I'm
learning new things everyday.

I can't talk, but I can have a conversation. I tell Mummy and Daddy what I need by signing and pointing to pictures.

I can't talk, but I am me.
Who else would I want to be?

Thank you for reading about me ♥

Made in the USA
Coppell, TX
18 April 2025